THE ROAD

Edwin Sánchez

I0140029

BROADWAY PLAY PUBLISHING INC
224 E 62nd St, NY, NY 10065
www.broadwayplaypub.com
info@broadwayplaypub.com

THE ROAD
© Copyright 2013 by Edwin Sánchez

First printing December 2013
I S B N: 978-0-88145-325-6

Book design: Marie Donovan
Page make-up: Adobe Indesign
Typeface: Palatino
Printed and bound in the U S A

THE ROAD received it's first full production in 1999
at the Clemente Soto Velez Cultural Center in New
York where it was produced by The Fourth Unity (Moe
Bertran, Producer). The cast and creative contributors
were:

RALPHY...Ivan Davila
CLARA... Ann Chandler
JACK ....Dennis Smith

Director... Antonio Merenda
Set design...Jason Archer
Sound design...Jason Scott
Lighting design ....Gregory Dralva
Technical director..David Guzzone
Publicist ....Ron Lasko
Assistant director.. Lisa Monahan

CHARACTERS & SETTING

RALPHY, *a man with AIDS, thirty-five*
CLARA, *his mother, fifty-five*
JACK, *his father, sixty-five*

Part of the stage will be JACK *and* CLARA's *kitchen. The other part of the stage will be a unit set that can represent the different stops along* RALPHY's *journey through America.*

This play is dedicated to Dennis Smith

(The light of a T V set is all the illumination in the room. The lights rise fully. RALPHY'*s bedroom. He is asleep. His mother,* CLARA, *is sitting in a chair next to him. She is watching her favorite soap opera,* Days of Our Lives. RALPHY *awakens suddenly.)*

RALPHY: *(Not fully awake)* Lucy.

CLARA: Just a second, honey. This is almost over.

RALPHY: *(Fully awake)* I want to see I Love Lucy.

CLARA: Just a second, honey.

RALPHY: *(Under his breath.)* I'm dying but God forbid she should miss a second of *Days of Our Lives*. That's important. Fuck me. I've got so much else going for me.

*(*CLARA *begins to cry. She uses the remote control to change the channel.)*

RALPHY: I'm sorry, mommy. You finish watching your show.

CLARA: No, it's okay. It's over.

RALPHY: Please, please put it back on.

CLARA: No, I want to see Lucy.

RALPHY: Why do you put up with me?

*(*JACK *enters.)*

JACK: Oh boy, I Love Lucy.

RALPHY: Daddy, you hate Lucy.

JACK: I love Lucy.

RALPHY: No, you don't.

JACK: Do you want me to hate it?

RALPHY: What?

JACK: If you do, I'll hate it. Just tell me what you want.

CLARA: Me, too. You're the gay of our lives.

JACK: And that's why you're dying.

CLARA: He is not dying. I'm sure they'll find a cure any day now.

JACK: Nobody's fault but your own. But don't worry, we'll be nice to you. We have to be. Until you die.

RALPHY: I'm dying as fast as I can.

JACK: By the way, how did you get AIDS? Bitten by a mosquito? You want to play gin rummy?

RALPHY: No. I want to play solitaire.

JACK: Double solitaire it is!

CLARA: Remember to let him win.

(RALPHY *pulls out a gun and shoots his father.*)

CLARA: That was a lovely shot, Ralphy.

(RALPHY *shoots* CLARA. *With the T V soundtrack in the background* RALPHY *puts the gun in his mouth.*)

(*Blackout*)

(*A shot is heard. Lights up. Both* CLARA *and* JACK *are applauding.*)

JACK: Finally. Finally.

CLARA: Is my baby happy now?

(RALPHY *shoots frantically at* CLARA *and* JACK, *who continue applauding.*)

(*Blackout*)

(Lights up. CLARA *and* JACK *enter the kitchen carrying groceries.* JACK *puts his bag on the counter, kisses the back of* CLARA*'s neck and exits. She begins to empty the bags and hits the "play" button on the telephone answering machine.)*

RALPHY: *(Voiceover)* Hi, this is Ralphy. I gotta go. I won't be back. My head's exploding. I keep having this dream of killing you both. You've been so nice to me. I'm so ashamed. I snap at you, I make you cry. I went to the doctor to get my medicine and I see this guy, just like me, smack his father. He cursed at him. And I knew why he did it. What do I do with this rage that is eating me up alive? I'm rambling. I love you both. I will not hurt you. I swear to God I will not hurt either of you. Goodbye.

(A beep is heard after the message. CLARA *stops the machine. She takes the tape out of the machine and breaks it any way she can. She stuffs a dish towel in her mouth and begins to scream. She begins to hit herself.)*

JACK: *(Voice off)* News is about to start.

*(*CLARA *tries to control herself.)*

JACK: *(Voice off)* Is there anything sweet in the kitchen? A cookie or something? *(He enters.)* You unpack the Oreos yet? Bet you they're at the bottom. Ralphy! You want to see the news down here?

CLARA: He's resting. Let him rest.

JACK: You've been crying.

CLARA: No.

JACK: What did he say to you now?

CLARA: Nothing. Go watch the news.

JACK: Look, he just can't talk to you any way he pleases.

CLARA: I'm okay. Watch the news.

JACK: I'm going upstairs to talk to him.

CLARA: He's asleep.

JACK: We can't do more than what we're doing for him.

RALPHY: They could not have done more for me.

JACK: Never enough.

RALPHY: Maybe too much.

CLARA: He gets angry, he takes it out on us. We're family. I wish I didn't get on his nerves. I should change.

JACK: We didn't do anything we have to apologize for. I know plenty of people who wouldn't have taken him back into their house.

CLARA: His home.

JACK: We are doing everything we can. He decides it's not enough, that's his problem. I didn't like what he was, but I made my peace with it. You tell me if we're so terrible. You tell me.

CLARA: How am I supposed to know!!

JACK: I don't know what I said or asked that gives you the right to talk to me that way.

CLARA: Please.

JACK: What?

CLARA: Please, get out of my sight. Get out of my sight! *(She picks up a kitchen chair by the back and bangs it on the floor for emphasis.)* Leave me alone. Get out of here.

(JACK turns to leave. CLARA rushes towards him and hugs him.)

CLARA: Please don't go.

RALPHY: I don't buy into this "you always hurt the one you love" crap.

CLARA: I'm sorry. I'm so sorry.

JACK: Sssh. I forgive you. It's okay. He'll hear you. You don't want him to hear you, do you, Clara?

RALPHY: How the hell am I supposed to hear her when I'm not even there? She's lying to make it all nice and neat.

JACK: I don't know that yet.

RALPHY: I'd be real curious to see how long she can keep you out of my room. Will she invite you to my funeral or are you just going to stumble upon my gravestone.

CLARA: Ralphy's doctor called. He said…he said Ralphy needed quiet and he is not to be disturbed for the next few days. He'll be back to normal in the next few days.

(Lights on RALPHY)

RALPHY: Dear folks, after I got out of the doctor's office I went to Fire Island. Visited some old haunts. Saw the place where I first slow danced with a guy. Went down to the beach. Made my peace with myself and lay down. The water woke me up today. Here I was hoping I was dead and God is raining on my parade. I'm sitting on the beach, feeling the rain on me. Still angry. Still empty. I can't go home 'cause I'll kill you, or you'll kill me or we'll kill each other. And I'm asking myself here, since I haven't got a hell of a lot of time left, what would I like to do? What would make Ralphy boy happy? I have always operated on what would make other people happy because that would make me a good little boy. But here and now, with the sands of time washing away, what would make Ralphy happy? I realize, I haven't got the faintest idea.

CLARA: He sent us a letter with no return address. I called all his friends, thinking maybe he might have told them what he wouldn't tell his parents. Nobody knows anything. Please tell me where you are. Don't go through this alone. That's what you have family for.

JACK: Ralphy come down today?

RALPHY: Don't lie to him.

CLARA: No.

JACK: Maybe he wants to play some gin rummy.

CLARA: Just let him sleep. He's so peaceful when he sleeps.

RALPHY: You're not going to tell him.

CLARA: You'll come back. I know you will.

RALPHY: Why can't I decide when it's over. Or if it's over. Or when I want it to be over.

(CLARA *exits and slams* RALPHY'*s bedroom door. She walks heavily to the back kitchen door and opens and closes it.*)

CLARA: Okay Ralphy. Take your time, sweetheart. You stay out as long as you like. Call me if you need anything. Anything at all.

RALPHY: What do you get the man who has everything?

(JACK *enters.*)

JACK: Was that Ralphy?

CLARA: He just left. His friend picked him up. They're going to the doctor and maybe a movie.

JACK: Haven't seen him in a week. When he comes back we should all sit down and have dinner together or maybe watch television.

RALPHY: Thursdays, when I was on my own, I would come over for dinner. You would cook pork chops and I would bitch about men in the kitchen with you and then I would go into the living room and bitch about work with dad. Then we'd have dinner in front of the

T V and watch a movie 'cause there was nothing the three of us could talk about.

CLARA: Oh honey, you know how Ralphy gets sometimes. The doctor just wants him to avoid stress. You'll see him soon.

RALPHY: Hocked my ring, my watch and my gold chain with the Saint Christopher medal. Bought myself a present. *(Takes out a gun)* One size fits all.

JACK: You think so?

CLARA: He might even call us while he's out. He loves us.

JACK: Are you running errands today?

CLARA: Yeah. Ralphy wanted some magazines and I've got to take some videos back for him.

JACK: I'll get them.

CLARA: No! You'll wake him.

JACK: He's at the doctor's office, remember?

CLARA: I'll get them.

JACK: Take them back later. I may want to watch them. Why don't you just go get his magazines?

CLARA: I love you. *(She exits.)*

JACK: You do, don't you Clara?

(JACK pulls out RALPHY's letter from his pocket and begins to read.)

RALPHY: Dear folks, I finally had to leave Fire Island. Too many memories. I was feeling so much at once I was numb. You ever get that way? My last night here I buried my medicine in the sand. And no, I am not being self destructive or yes, I am being self destructive. In either case, I'm not going to be able to die with you both looking over my shoulder. You just can't let go. How much do you both want to hit me? I want to hit you both. It got to the point where I couldn't stand the sight of either one of you. I hated you both so much. I hear San Francisco is nice this time of year.

(JACK *crumples up the letter and puts it in the ashtray. He sets it on fire.*)

RALPHY: Ashes to ashes.

JACK: Your mother never lied to me before.

RALPHY: Dust to dust.

JACK: When you lost your job, who lent you money? When you lost your apartment who took you in? And you hate us? You hate us?

RALPHY: Yeah.

(JACK *storms offstage. Enter* CLARA.)

CLARA: Did you burn something? Were you cooking?

(*Enter* JACK *carrying a cardboard box.*)

JACK: Do you know where he is?

CLARA: Who? What have you got in the box?

JACK: I'm asking you a question. Do you know where he is?

(CLARA *looks in the box.*)

CLARA: This is Ralphy's stuff. He's gonna need it when he comes home.

(JACK *knocks the box out of* CLARA's *hands.*)

JACK: I asked you, do you know where he is?

CLARA: No.

JACK: Okay then.

(JACK *exits and returns with another box.*)

CLARA: Why are you packing this up? He'll need it when he comes back.

JACK: Ralphy's not coming back. He hates us, hates everything we've ever done for him. Our son runs away and you don't even tell me?

CLARA: He's coming back.

JACK: I'm burning this stuff. This stuff is trash.

CLARA: Please don't.

JACK: Don't touch them!

CLARA: Why do you want to break my heart? Why do you both want to break my heart?

(As JACK *carries out the boxes,* CLARA *begins to write* RALPHY.*)*

CLARA: Ralphy, where are you? Tell us what to do, please, we will do whatever you say.

*(*CLARA *tries to cover the letter when* JACK *reenters. He wrests it from her.)*

CLARA: I'm not finished. Give me that.

JACK: Do you know where to send it?

CLARA: No.

JACK: Then what are you going to do? Put it in a bottle? Take out a full page ad in one of those gay magazines and hope he reads it?

CLARA: I don't know.

RALPHY: I have decided to become a gay guerrilla commando. Picture this, on my way to San Francisco I make a pit stop in Washington, D C and kill Jesse Helms. Pandemonium. I off a few supreme court justices and take a few T V evangelists as hostages. I become the most wanted man in America. Or I may henna my hair. Decisions. Decisions.

JACK: Why don't you tell him you haven't slept since he's been gone? That you haven't eaten. You want to drive yourself crazy? You got no place to send him this letter. He doesn't want to know from us. He hates us. What does it take for you to realize he doesn't want us?

RALPHY: Dear folks, having a wonderful time, glad you're not here.

CLARA: Dear Ralphy, I am very angry with you. I know that writing this to you is useless, but maybe I won't self-destruct if I do this. I've gotten your last...your most recent letter and I hope you keep writing. I'd do just about anything if you would call; but I guess that's not gonna happen, right? Your father has been very supportive...your father has been very supportive...I hate you.

(Enter JACK.*)*

JACK: Another letter to Ralphy?

CLARA: I'm telling him I hate him.

*(*JACK *goes behind her and kisses her head.)*

RALPHY: I didn't dream about killing you and daddy last night. Good sign.

CLARA: I am going to keep writing you. And some day, God willing, I will be able to send my letters to you. Please don't lock me out.

(Lights up on JACK *sitting in a chair reading a letter.)*

RALPHY: Dear Daddy, walking in Jersey today I saw a boy with his father washing the family car. Kid couldn't have been more than seven. Took everything so seriously until his father wets him with the hose. He squeals, sounds just like a girl, but this is happening before he's had a chance to edit himself. Father and son in a messy water fight. Little kid sees me and aims the hose at me, he's laughing. Father stops him. I go on. I would have given anything to get wet. I love you, daddy.

(JACK *crumples up the letter and tosses it on the floor.* CLARA *rises and straightens out the letter.*)

JACK: Where are you going with that?

RALPHY: She has a secret place, daddy, where she keeps your love letters and mine.

JACK: That's mine.

CLARA: You hate him.

JACK: I don't hate him. I don't. I don't!

CLARA: I am so mad right now I could spit bullets. You know that stupid Mrs Tyler? Got an opinion on everything even if she doesn't know anything about it. She starts by telling me, "Well, you'll excuse my honesty, Clara, but no one can tell me that AIDS is not a punishment from God. Now, I know your son..." And that's as far as she got 'cause I grabbed a hold of her moussed hair and I would not let go. Your father had to come out and separate us. And I told him, "Jack, get your hands off me. Because after I finish killing her, I'll kill you." Your father dragged me inside and gave me some tranquilizers. And I was thinking, just as the pills began to take effect, "Why do they want to numb you when you finally start to feel?"

RALPHY: Dear folks, every time I get to a scenic place I lie down and try it out for size. Oh, there's been a slight change. No more gay guerrilla commando. I'm now holding out for Malibu. Look, you've got to be flexible in life. What the fuck ever possessed me to bury my medicine in the sand? Felt like shit today, but it finally passed. Maybe I'll have to pull a job, get some more medicine. "Stick 'em up", with a nylon over my head. Sandal toe? Taupe?

CLARA: Shut up! This is not a big joke here. My son is dying! Okay? This is not something I want to find humor in. You talk about my denial, what do you think you're doing?

RALPHY: Well, mom, I'm praying I don't go nuts. And if discussing shades of hosiery does it for me, I think that's just what I'll do. "Your son is dying?" Gee, do I know him? Maybe he's the same guy who when he found out he had AIDS went down to the East River and cried his guts out? Yeah, I kind of remember him. I'm all cried out. What's going to get me to Malibu, besides my winning smile, is the trip itself. I want it to take a long time. The longer it takes, the longer I got.

CLARA: Your father was in a rampage the other day. Couldn't find his reading glasses. So I took his hand and said, "Calm down, I'll read the letter to you."

JACK: How do I know you won't leave anything out?

CLARA: I won't.

JACK: Things that would hurt.

CLARA: I'll read them.

JACK: Or embarrass me.

CLARA: I'll read them.

JACK: Or make me so angry. Angry all over again at him for disappearing.

CLARA: 'Cause it wouldn't be right if I left anything out. So your father sat down and we held hands as I read your letter.

JACK: Afterwards she asked me to mail her reply. And I looked at her and said, "Mail? Mail the hell where?" Well, she put her hands on her hips like she'll sometimes do and gave me one of her evil looks. Then her face lightens up and she says…

CLARA: Oh, yeah.

RALPHY: Dear folks, well, here's the goddamn cherry on my cake, I got mugged last night. I'm like trying to pull out my gun, block the blows and call for the police all at the same time. Had the shit kicked out of me, but they didn't get my gun. No siree, Bob. I was a real man, Jack. I think I shot one of them in the foot. Gotta run, what's the point?

CLARA: It is what it is?

RALPHY: You're learning, mom.

(Night. CLARA is looking out of the kitchen window at the rain. Enter JACK.)

JACK: Clara?

CLARA: Don't turn on the lights.

(Silence. JACK embraces CLARA from the back.)

JACK: How long have you been there?

CLARA: I wonder if it's raining where he is. Is he indoors or outdoors? Has he eaten?

(RALPHY is hitchhiking. A car passes him by.)

RALPHY: Goodbye asshole number nine hundred seventy six.

JACK: It's a vicious world out there and sometimes I feel I didn't do enough to get you ready for it. I apologize. I know you probably don't want to hear this but have you thought about going to church? Getting reborn or something along those lines. Might make your…transition easier. I've been going every night.

RALPHY: I've been thinking a lot about God.

JACK: I was not a churchgoer before, and for that, dear God, I am truly regretful.

RALPHY: I haven't been reborn or anything, but I think of him in a different way. For one thing I hope he exists.

JACK: I pray for you. I even light candles for you.

RALPHY: He exists.

JACK: I ask him to watch out for my Ralphy boy.

RALPHY: I hope, I hope, I hope.

JACK: Maybe someday God will let me know why it was my son and not me. It just doesn't seem fair. Old people die first. That's the rule.

CLARA: Dear Ralphy, yesterday, for the first time in I don't know when I went out and bought myself a new dress. And I had my hair set and styled. I wanted to look pretty. I felt a little foolish, but I got over it. Your father hasn't touched me in six years. You know what I mean. I'm not sure I miss it; I mean we still cuddle. But, …I guess the part I miss the most is being desired.

RALPHY: I tie a rope around my waist to hold my pants up.

CLARA: I undress in the dark so he won't see my body and then I get angry at myself. For heaven's sake. I shouldn't be embarrassed when I'm naked in front of him. I am a fifty-five year old woman; I have the body I have earned. I have given birth, nursed, miscarried and worked side by side with him. That's the body he should see. His partner's body. Why doesn't he want it? Can't he just pretend?

RALPHY: (Sings) If you want my body
And you think I'm sexy
Come on baby, let me know
(Spoken) I was always a horny boy.

JACK: The boys still at it?

CLARA: Yeah, Ralphy said not to disturb them while they were studying.

JACK: He has a lot more friends this semester.

RALPHY: Why shouldn't I? I put out. Dated the high school jock, who in turn married the high school jockette, giving birth to a whole slew of little jockeys. Do you know he still called me, even after he was married?

JACK: He's one of the guys now.

RALPHY: A man's man. Sometimes I find myself lying in a strange place and it's dark and my hand helps me remember. I miss the touch of someone. But I know married people who miss the touch of someone.

(CLARA *exhales loudly.*)

JACK: *(Softly)* Yes.

RALPHY: My hand is nice, but it's my hand. I want to feel someone's breath on me. Yeah, right there. What do you say next letter we swap losing virginity stories?

JACK: Are you crazy?! How stupid can you be?!

CLARA: What's this?

JACK: You always feel better after you write Ralphy. I'm writing him a letter.

(CLARA *reads from* JACK's *letter.*)

CLARA: "Are you crazy?! How stupid can you be?!" This is why he won't give us a return address.

RALPHY: I met someone on the road. This guy who's doing what I'm doing. Only he's been at it for the last twenty five years. Hoboing. He told me his story and I told him mine. I lied. I was finally the lawyer you wanted me to be. Or did I say astronaut? I was funny, charming and after I was finished he asked me, "What are you so angry about?" Do I have it written on my forehead, "I am pissed"? So I backtracked. How much do I want to tell this guy? My mother sold candy at Woolworth's on Fordham road in the Bronx.

CLARA: *(Wearing a red smock)* It's almost three o'clock, can you take over for me Rachel? Hey, now look, if it makes my Ralphy popular to bring some of his little school friends over to see his mother and get some free candy, so what? It's not like I don't pay for it. Makes him popular. Ever since he brings them here they stopped picking on him. My Ralphy has lots of friends. Of course they'll like him when I stop working here. Why shouldn't they?

RALPHY: My father was an accountant.

JACK: *(In a jacket and tie)* This is my son. Say hello Ralphy. Shake Mister Green's hand. All of twelve. Yeah, well, he's not much into sports, but he loves numbers. Don't you Ralphy boy? He's going to be an accountant just like his old man. No, he's not going to be in anybody's way today. He's just going to sit here and read. He likes to read. All the secretaries have come over and pinched his cheek. He's going to be a real lady killer. Well, yeah he is a little fat. I'm going to take him to the park and we'll play some sport, sometime soon. Nice talking to you, sir. There, Ralphy boy, goes a sorry excuse for a man. Why? Couldn't you tell?

RALPHY: I was an accountant. I hated it. Hated numbers. Let's see, slept with the boss, he was married. We pushed the pictures of the wife and kids off the desk so it's not like they could see. Had the same job for nine years. Lived at home until I was twenty two, got my own apartment. Nothing exciting. Came out to my parents when I was thirty. I find it hard to believe they didn't know. You know, you're thirty years old and you still haven't met the "right" girl. My mother started to cry, but I stopped her. "No, these are my tears, mommy. But thanks anyway." My father was shaving, and as I'm telling him I'm thinking, "How stupid am I, telling a man with a razor that his only son is gay"? They got over it, I guess. I kind of miss them. I wonder who they miss. And in the middle of all this friendly chit chat I reached out and grabbed the hobo's arm. "How do you deal with the loneliness? With this aloneness that's in every part of you." And he changed the subject. "Aren't the stars beautiful?", he asked. They were. I guess then and there they were all that mattered.

JACK: Are you telling me I could have been a hero to my son had I deserted the family and lived among hobos? Then I would have been exciting. Then I would have been some father.

CLARA: You didn't hear a word he said, did you?

JACK: What he just said was that he'd rather be with a hobo than with me. Us.

RALPHY: Spare change, nickels, dimes, quarters. Spare change. Oh yeah, sir, I'll be sure to get a job real soon. Dear folks, Boston is so historic. Must dash.

CLARA: Why didn't you ever come to me?

RALPHY: There's a conversation I'd love to hear. "Gee, mom, I think I'm gay."

JACK: I should have taken you to the park to play catch.

RALPHY: I was a very cute child, wasn't I?

CLARA: You were always so quiet as a kid.

JACK: Always did his homework the second he got home.

CLARA: Hated to see us fight. A good boy.

JACK: Straight As.

RALPHY: I was an average student.

JACK: In all your years in school, I was never called in because of trouble. Not once. We could trust you. Always thought of others first.

CLARA: What's it like to be totally on your own? You don't have to answer to anyone. You come and go as you please. When I was a little girl I was taught that was selfish.

RALPHY: So?

CLARA: One summer I was visiting my grandmother in Fredricksburg, Virginia. I remember cutting all my hair off so I could play with the boys and go swimming. I did it myself; got such a whipping. My mother cried, she said that was the only pretty thing about me.

RALPHY: So?

CLARA: So it was selfish.

RALPHY: I always used to have this fantasy about you, mommy. That I would call you and tell you that I was coming into town to visit you. And you would tell me that you were too busy, your life was so full, you were too busy. I always wanted you to have a life of your own and friends of your own, you just never did. Nix Malibu. I have decided that it's just too frivolous for me. What will I do? The world is mine for the taking. P S: Felt too weak to move for three days. Scratch that …I'm fine. How are you? That's nice.

CLARA: Tell me the truth! Everything cannot be great. Stop sending me postcards telling me how perfect everything is.

JACK: Maybe he's all right.

CLARA: He's dying, Jack. Where have you been?

RALPHY: I definitely would have recast that last exchange. It's odd what time does to memory. I look back and realize that I didn't prize the genuine. Too busy chasing the next sensation. The one that would be the best ever and would prove to everyone that I must be the best ever, too. I know now that I never had anyone love me like my ex, Javier, did. So why wasn't it enough? I preferred to pursue the man who would break my heart. I was always such a coward when it came to danger but I was a daredevil when it came to my heart. Always preferring to love without a net. And if I fell, which I always did, I loved the fall. I might as well have taken a hammer to my heart. Break it and piece it together. How many times can you play that game? After a while it takes more and more effort to put a heart together again, and it always seems like there's a piece missing. God, I hate it when I get like this. So, tell me, are you two guys always happy you married? No regrets? I'm sure.

JACK: It is what it is. Nothing is going to be perfect all the time. That's impossible.

CLARA: Impossible.

JACK: But that's the person who's going to be there when you need them most. And you'll be there for them.

CLARA: And you'll always remember what made them special to you. How Old Spice and Evening in Paris mixed so well.

JACK: Ralphy was twenty five.

CLARA: Ten years ago.

JACK: He took us out to the Venetian Room for our anniversary. Picked out the flowers I was supposed to give you.

CLARA: Helped me pick out a dress...

RALPHY: Blue was always your color, mom.

CLARA: ...and got my hair done at some fancy, over priced place.

JACK: Got us a table in the corner.

CLARA: With him sitting two tables away.

JACK: Told us what we had to order.

RALPHY: I suggested.

JACK: I wanted steak.

RALPHY: You can have steak anywhere. This is a deluxe French restaurant. Besides, it wouldn't have gone with the champagne.

CLARA: He was so excited for us.

JACK: He's picked the restaurant, the meal, the wine. At one point he gets up from his table and tells me I should hold her hand. Practically pushes me out on the dance floor with his mother.

CLARA: It was like we didn't know how to go out without his help.

RALPHY: I wanted it to be special.

CLARA: You gave me earrings.

RALPHY: You gave me cuff links.

CLARA: Ralphy picked them both out. He always knew what I wanted.

JACK: What the heck does that mean?

CLARA: Hell. What the hell does that mean.

JACK: I know how to talk. I'm not the one with the towel in my mouth so no one will hear me scream. I know why you get undressed in the dark, too. It's so I won't see the bruises you get when you hit yourself. I'm not the one who's trying to hold this all in.

CLARA: Who do I got to talk to? If I cry it's bad and if I don't cry it's just as bad.

RALPHY: I hope I didn't open up a can of worms. I was just curious.

JACK: I know all about your curiousity.

RALPHY: Got picked up by a trucker. He wanted a blow job. I said, sure. I hit a big town. Chicago. Trucker got us a room in a motel. I got cleaned up and when he went out to get us some beers I beat it. He wasn't really my type anyway. I had a few bucks I had saved so I go to a gay bar. Thank God for careful lighting. No gay bar should ever be without it. Everyone checking you out the second you walk in. I feel lightheaded just being in this atmosphere again. This crazy song is on and I look up and there's this guy on the dance floor with his arms extended in my direction! This is nuts. This dance could set me back six weeks. But I find myself going in his direction. Following the smile of enjoyment. I stop. Let him come to me. He buys me a drink. Gin and tonic. Jimmy. He's twenty eight, a store manager and has curly blond hair. I find myself making jokes and he's laughing. He doesn't see tombstones when he looks into my eyes. He takes a sip from my glass and I almost stop him. Me, and if anyone should know how AIDS is transmitted it's me. I let him drink. God, he has the sexiest mouth I've ever seen on any human being. A romantic song comes on and he's pulling me by my hand and we're on the dance floor before I know it. It's cold. He takes my face in his hand and kisses me full on the mouth. He pulls away and tries to look at me seductively, but I pull him back. I want to be held. I want to be desired. Those feelings in me have not died.

CLARA: Like mother like son.

RALPHY: The warmth of his body is intoxicating.

CLARA: This treasure he has in his arms.

RALPHY: His breath is caressing my eyelids.

CLARA: He's telling you how special you are.

RALPHY: I don't think I've ever been held at a better time than now. Maybe I have found my answer. Maybe it wasn't as difficult as I thought.

JACK: Everybody wants to be loved, but you think a stranger is the answer? How can you go into raptures over someone who's last name you don't even know? What? Do you meet someone tomorrow who's the new answer?

RALPHY: Gee thanks, Pops, for putting everything in perspective.

JACK: You're a man, right? Then take responsibility-

RALPHY: Hold it right there. I have always taken responsibility for my actions. You think I have AIDS 'cause I went out and got AIDS.

JACK: I never said that.

RALPHY: I got news for you, you never said much of anything.

JACK: Okay, so help me understand. How did you get it?

RALPHY: How do you think?

JACK: I want you to tell me. Were you in church?

RALPHY: If you mean was I doing it with the altar boys, the answer is no. At least not anymore.

JACK: So tell me who I should blame. No, I'm serious, tell me who I can go beat up. Whose fault is it you're dying? Is it mine, is it your mother's? Whose the hell is it? You point them out to me. Who did this to my Ralphy?

RALPHY: What are you going to do, Jack? Kill every man I ever slept with?

JACK: Maybe I'm the worst father in the world but-

RALPHY: Are you all of a sudden going to try to understand what my life has been about? Better late than never, huh. You're looking for somebody to blame? How about me. I am guilty of hard ons, wet dreams and desire. Something you couldn't possibly understand, right Jack?

JACK: You had a choice. Nobody put a gun to your head and said, "do it".

RALPHY: You're right, that was my choice. And when I die it won't be because I tried to be Jack II, the sequel.. I'm dying as Ralphy boy. Ralph Miller. My own man. Every choice I made I take full responsibility for. Can you say the same thing, Mr. Man. It's okay if you say you hate me. I already know it.

JACK: That's not true.

RALPHY: Don't perjure yourself, Jack. Never lie to the dying. God lets us read minds, it's sort of a trade off. What's the outcome here, Jack? I'm trying to pick up the tempo here, pops. Work with me, work with me. Don't you wish I was dead? Don't you wish I would hurry up and die?

JACK: I wish you weren't dying. Once before you die I'd like to sleep with you. Wrap you in my arms and hold you. That's what I wish.

(JACK *begins to cry.* CLARA *comforts him.*)

CLARA & RALPHY: I know, I know.

RALPHY: I got some Kaposi Sarcoma lesions on my face. Got the first one last Friday. Got seven or eight now all over my body. I try not to look in store windows. I don't want to die ugly. Isn't that vain? Isn't that foolish? I hate how people look at me on the street. They all know now. Am I being paranoid? What's next? Dementia? Blindness? What happens if I go blind? I'm not going home. I'll kill myself first. I'm not going home.

CLARA: Every letter is proof that he's alive. And what happens when the letters stop? First week, I'll say the mail is slow. After two weeks I'll say it got lost in the mail. By the third week I'll refuse to discuss it. I live from letter to letter and so does he. What if either of us died, he wouldn't even know.

RALPHY: You wouldn't dare upstage me.

CLARA: How does he manage, day to day?

JACK: He wouldn't even go camping with me because he wouldn't shit in the woods. What's he doing now?

RALPHY: Shitting in the woods. I've had quite an education. I know how to panhandle now, didn't know that before. How to steal a bum's shoes while he sleeps, 'cause I need them more. How to survive sleeping in a men's shelter. How to make the most out of any food you get. How to live without guilt. That was the big one. There was a time in my life where I was embarrassed to be me, 'cause I thought you were both embarrassed that I was who I was. Now I am shame free. I am no one's disappointment and no one's responsibility.

JACK: That's never totally true.

RALPHY: Can you spare some change for a gentleman to get something to eat? Have a nice day. Dear folks, I met a very nice family here in uh, ...Lexington, Kentucky. There was a big tornado coming and they insisted I stay with them. There was the mama and the papa and little Georgie. They shared their food, their chairs and their beds with me. One bed was too hard, the other one was too soft, but little Georgie's bed was just right.

JACK: He's just told us the story of Goldilocks and the Three Bears. Ralphy, if you're going to write, tell us the truth.

RALPHY: That's exactly how it happened. Hey, look, I was there. People love me. They were a good Christian family and in the eyes of their Lord they had no choice. Both cried the entire time I was there. Kept a can of Lysol at easy reach to clean any surface I happened to touch. Gave me food and a blanket they insisted I keep 'cause they'll never use it again. They'd sooner burn it. That's not what they said, but that's what they meant. When it gets cold I pretend my blanket is a mink cape. *(He poses with blanket.)* I would have made a very good diva.

CLARA: Your father had a dream about you last night.

JACK: Your mother had a dream about you last night.

RALPHY: I always wanted to be a realist, but dreams get in my way. *(He curls himself up in a ball.)*

CLARA: You're six years old and I catch you playing with dolls and instead of telling your father-

RALPHY: Which you did.

CLARA: I sit down and play with you. And when your father comes home he sits down and plays with us, too. And from that moment on you trust us. Forever.

JACK: It was the first time I saw you. Day you were born. I remember holding you so gently. You turned to look at me and you started talking. High brow stuff. Voicing opinions, discussing world affairs. I'm walking around the hospital with you, proud as all get out. Showing all the other fathers that my son can talk. What the hell can theirs do? Then all of a sudden you turn to me and say, "Of course you know, I am a homosexual." And I drop you. As if I'd been burnt. I always…your mother always wakes up before you hit the floor.

RALPHY: Forgive the paper. I couldn't find anything to write on. I think someone must have wrapped a skunk in this. Paper and pencil are usually easy to come by. Stamps are a drag. I've got to buy them or steal them. I had to write you today. It's my birthday. I am not going to be depressed. I am celebrating, and if I know mommy she has already cried three times since she got up. She is sitting in front of a birthday cake and will begin to get teary as she reads this.

(CLARA *is indeed sitting in front of a birthday cake.*)

RALPHY: Go for it, mommy.

(CLARA *wipes the tears form her eyes and digs into the cake with her hands.*)

RALPHY: Did you have any candles on it?

(CLARA *shakes her head no.*)

RALPHY: I'm thirty six.

(CLARA *lifts a handful of cake and toasts him.*)

RALPHY: Be happy for me. I didn't think I would make it to thirty six. I sent you both birthday cards that I hope make you laugh. Tried to picture both of you laughing. Couldn't do it. Realized how long it's been since either one of you laughed. Hope there have been some laughs while I've been gone.

(*Enter* JACK.)

JACK: You're going to make yourself sick if you eat that whole cake.

RALPHY: Ask him how church was.

CLARA: How was church?

JACK: You should have come.

RALPHY: Shrug.

(CLARA *does.*)

JACK: Today's his birthday.

CLARA: I know.

RALPHY: And the greatest gift either of you can give me is to just be happy.

JACK: Do you want to go out for dinner, tonight? After you finish dessert I mean.

CLARA: Fuck you.

(JACK *tenses.*)

JACK: I see we're having rum cake.

RALPHY: Mom, never turn down a meal with a man. Haven't I taught you anything?

(JACK *picks up a fork and sits next to* CLARA.)

JACK: May I?

RALPHY: All of a sudden, he's Cary Grant.

(CLARA *nods and smiles.*)

CLARA: I was hoping he would call today.

JACK: I was hoping he would be home today. I was hoping that I would come home from church and there he'd be. Only like he used to be. The old Ralphy.

RALPHY: There was no straight Ralphy, daddy. This always seems to confuse you. Feed her some cake and go upstairs and make mad and passionate love. Hell, do it right there on the table.

CLARA: I wonder what Ralphy's doing right now.

RALPHY: Don't talk about me, for God's sake, make a move.

CLARA: Dear Ralphy, your father took me out dancing to celebrate your birthday. He sees me sitting in front of this cake I made and told me we're going out. And he takes me out. Like on a date. He bought me flowers and we had dinner out and then we went dancing. I cannot remember the last time I went dancing.

(CLARA *and* JACK *begin to dance.*)

JACK: So yesterday on your birthday, I decided we would have a date that you would be proud of and we could enjoy.

RALPHY: I always wished you were more romantic with each other.

JACK: Your mother could have had her pick of any boy she wanted.

RALPHY: And you wanted Jack?

CLARA: I wanted Peter. Who didn't want me. Then I wanted Keith, who also didn't want me. I think your father was more in love when we married than I was, but…I liked him a lot.

RALPHY: Not even second choice?

CLARA: Maybe I should have held out. I grew to love him. And I had you. My baby with the too, too sad eyes.

RALPHY: Was Clara your first choice?

JACK: More or less.

RALPHY: I wish you guys were more romantic about this.

JACK: What's romance done for you?

CLARA: Jack.

JACK: It's true. He talks about the damned thing as if it were some cure all.

RALPHY: Sorry. So you had a date on my birthday. That's nice.

JACK: It was.

RALPHY: Did you enjoy yourselves?

CLARA: Oh yeah.

RALPHY: What time were you home by?

CLARA: Oh, we were home watching T V by, I guess eleven thirty.

JACK: What does that have to do with anything?

RALPHY: Just asking. Why is it okay for you to judge my life but it doesn't work the other way around?

JACK: I am not going to talk to you if you choose to speak that way. You do not exist.

RALPHY: A little touchy, huh Jack?

JACK: Your mother and I had the real thing.

RALPHY: If you mean you could go into restaurants, hold hands in public and not have to worry about some asshole making faggot jokes, then yeah, you and mom had the real thing. I'm standing there and this guy tells his date, "check out the faggot", I turn and say, "First of all, it's Mister Faggot to you. And secondly, is there anything else you'd like to say to my face as opposed to my back?" His girlfriend gasps, he is speechless. I continue on my way. I'm shaking. Am I nuts? This guy could have killed me. Right, like I got a lot to lose.

JACK: When you were a little boy I would pick you up and you would say—

RALPHY: When I grow up I want to be just like you. Do you want to be just like me, daddy? Could you be just like me.?

(Enter CLARA she is wearing a kerchief over her head.)

CLARA: Don't be mad.

JACK: What is it?

CLARA: (Taking off her kerchief to reveal her hair has been cut.) I just wanted to see what it looked like.

JACK: What have you done to yourself? You had no right. We didn't discuss this.

CLARA: I didn't want to.

JACK: It looks terrible.

CLARA: I know. But it's my terrible.

RALPHY: Dear folks, this is the story how good luck turned to bad luck turned to heroics turned to I don't know what. I found a twenty in the trash while I was looking for a midnight snack. Decided what I needed more than anything else in the world was…to shop. I'm in Orange County, California, mall capital of the free world and a long way from Riverside Drive. I have dramatically draped my mink blanket over my shoulders and I pretend the lesions on my face are beauty marks. Right, Ralphy boy. People are looking at you because you are so beautiful. I decide to go into every single store, because I'm a consumer and proud of it. Kaybee Toys, second floor, near Nordstrom, proved my downfall. Walk in, not looking for trouble, and I find myself in the doll aisle. There is a twelve year old boy. He's looking at a Barbie doll. He doesn't dare touch it. His face. Well, he'd give anything just to touch her. I smile at him and pick her up. "Isn't she pretty?", I say. That sort of gives him permission and he picks one up, too. He is lost in his dream girl, when his parents call.

(CLARA and JACK assume the roles of the parents.)

JACK: Jerry!

CLARA: We're leaving, Jerry. Hurry up.

RALPHY: He holds on to her for an extra second and puts her back. I grab the doll, pay for her and take her to him. "Here, Jerry. I always wanted one when I was your age."

JACK: Get that thing away from my boy.

RALPHY: Jerry is turning a couple of shades of red here and I try to finesse my way out of it. "Look, it's just a gift." Father knocks Barbie out of my hands.

JACK: Not for my boy it isn't.

RALPHY: I pick her up. "Shouldn't Jerry decide that?" The mother knocks her out of my hands.

CLARA: Mister, don't rile my husband.

RALPHY: Rile? Who the fuck says "rile"? I pick up Barbie again, who's hair by now is a fright. "Look, your kid wants her. Deal with it." Jerry begins to cry. *He* knocks her out of my hands. And this is where it gets screwed. The father is about to deck me, when I pull out my gun. "Okay, nobody fucking move!" The mall is quiet now. "You, Jerry, pick up Barbie!" I look around, taking in the sea of humanity. I realize I'm as trapped as I'm ever going to be. The mall SWAT team walkie talkies itself into place. Do I take a human shield? Make a break for it? What have I done? All for the love of an eleven and a half inch woman who can't wear flats. But, she's been a true friend. Yes, she has. I hear someone whisper, "I think he has AIDS," and pretty soon AIDS is echoing all around me. "Hey, I got a gun!" And an audience. "A gun, see?" Who am I telling, me or them? The police start moving in for me and I introduce them as "The Fabulous Ralphy Boy Dancers!" I am about to be jumped and subdued by eight men in uniform and while I have fantasized about dates like this, reality is a sad substitute. I put the gun in my mouth, everyone freezes. I take it out, they move. In, freeze. Out, move. This is a bad Bugs Bunny cartoon. With the gun in my mouth I head to the information booth with the P A system. I must address my followers. All eyes are on me. "I want...I want...I want a complete makeover!"

JACK: Ralphy boy.

RALPHY: I'm dying here, folks.

CLARA: My poor baby.

RALPHY: I mean my jokes, mom. My jokes are dying.
No, I mean me. Look, when I was growing up I always
thought that I was the only gay person in the world.
Now I hear that at least ten percent of the population
is gay. Okay. Ten percent. So I want every gay here to
raise his or her hand or I'll blow the top of my head off.
I mean it. Raise your hand. All I want to know is that
I'm not the only one. People, people everywhere and
not a drop to drink. I put the gun down and raise my
hand. There is a brief pause. Possession of an illegal
weapon, reckless endangerment, resisting arrest (crock
of shit) and causing a riot. My public defender stressed
my extreme mental anguish and a deal was struck.
My liberty for five thousand dollars. I don't have five
thousand dollars. "Then I guess you'll have to serve
some time." What Perky Mason doesn't get is that time
I got even less of. I need five thousand dollars. I need it
wired to the jail here and I need you both not to come
out here or try to call me. I need you both to be my
friend. Please. I don't want to see you and I don't want
to talk to you. Something is happening to me right now
where my traveling companion is becoming the man of
my dreams. And if I come home, I'll make sure to bring
him. In the meantime, you've got me over a barrel.

CLARA: Let's go get him.

RALPHY: If you get me this I'll never ask for anything
else again.

CLARA: They're not going to take care of him in there.
He's not taking care of himself.

JACK: If we go there what's going to happen?

RALPHY: I'm not going to want to see you.

JACK: He's not going to want to see us.

CLARA: They have to release him to us. We're paying for him. He's ours.

RALPHY: I'm mine.

JACK: Maybe we should call him first.

RALPHY: If you do this for me I'll be your best friend.

JACK: Ask him if it's okay.

CLARA: You can come and go whenever you like.

JACK: We won't say anything.

CLARA: Just once before I die I would like to see my son again.

RALPHY: I love you, mom, but don't try to guilt the dying.

JACK: He can't get upset over a little phone call.

RALPHY: You have no idea what I can and will get upset over.

JACK: It's five thousand dollars, Ralphy boy.

CLARA: I just want to know you're okay.

JACK: We could get on the next plane.

CLARA: Bring you back with us until you're strong enough to go out again.

RALPHY: Mommy, can I go out and play?

CLARA: You could sleep in your own bed. Wouldn't you like that?

JACK: A face to face for five thousand dollars seems pretty fair to me.

RALPHY: What if I chose jail over seeing you two. Over talking to you two. Would that offend you?

JACK: Yes.

CLARA: It would cut through my heart like a knife.

RALPHY: Good.

CLARA: You don't mean that.

JACK: Why do we have to be kept at an arm's distance?

RALPHY: You must allow an old young man his dreams.

JACK: I go to church and pray that God will let me see you one more time. And that I'll be able to tell you what I should have, that I'll make it right.

RALPHY: You did okay.

CLARA: Then let us see you.

(RALPHY *steps over to the side of the stage where* CLARA *and* JACK *are. He looks healthy and strong.* CLARA *and* JACK *at first circle him before they hug him.* RALPHY *kisses both of his parents goodbye before going back to his side.)*

RALPHY: If you saw me now, all you would see would be AIDS. You wouldn't see any of the things I'm proud of. You wouldn't see the things I wanted you to see. You wouldn't see a man, you would see your son, who's dying.

CLARA: If we give you the money, will you call us?

JACK: He could have called us to ask for it, Clara. He's not going to call us.

RALPHY: Maybe I shouldn't have written to you. Keeping you as a part of my life if it would only be on my terms. Maybe I shouldn't write you again.

JACK: Dear Ralphy, we took the money to the jail.

CLARA: This is the hardest thing I have ever done in my entire life.

JACK: We will not force you to see us or talk to us. This is what you have chosen. And even though we don't always understand your rationale we will try to abide it.

CLARA: I hope they give you this package and I hope you open it. It's just a couple of sweaters and some pants. A new pair of sneakers and a few shirts.

JACK: There's some money tucked into the pants pockets. I hope no one steals it.

CLARA: Some underwear and a knapsack. Your father wanted to include a credit card.

JACK: We would just pay it. We wouldn't track you down by the bills or anything like that.

CLARA: I'm also including the letters I've been writing you.

JACK: Mine, too.

CLARA: Give you an idea of how we kept our sanity.

JACK: We asked the people in the jail about you.

CLARA: You're quite a little celebrity.

JACK: They wanted to tell you we were there.

CLARA: What kind of parents are you?

JACK: They had you in isolation. Solitary. Whatever.

CLARA: They asked us if we wanted to see you.

JACK: If we wanted.

CLARA: And I couldn't get the words out of my mouth to say, "He doesn't want to see us."

JACK: They gave us a lecture.

CLARA: On what bad parents we are.

JACK: "Don't you know your son is dying?"

CLARA: Possibly dying.

JACK: "Don't you care?"

CLARA: I really didn't feel like explaining myself to strangers.

JACK: We waited outside, Ralphy.

CLARA: We did.

JACK: Waited outside while they did your paperwork.

CLARA: "Aren't you people gonna take him home with you? Home is where he belongs."

JACK: Just give him the box, please.

(CLARA *and* JACK *set out a box for* RALPHY.)

CLARA: We held hands. Held each other up is more like it.

JACK: Every time the door would open I'd have to hold myself back.

CLARA: Then you came out.

JACK: Quite a shock. Quite a shock.

CLARA: You didn't look half bad.

JACK: You looked around when you got outside.

CLARA: Your father thought you were looking for us. Me? I just think you were glad to be free.

JACK: What would have happened if we ran up to you? If we'd thrown our arms around you.

CLARA: You walked right past us.

JACK: Moving kind of slow there, son.

CLARA: You didn't look half bad.

JACK: We were going to follow you for a ways, but...

CLARA: I told Jack we would have followed you to the ends of the earth.

JACK: You looked nice and clean, Ralphy.

CLARA: Going God knows where. Bet you don't even know.

JACK: See what kind of mischief you can get yourself into now.

(RALPHY *rummages through the box until he finds the letters his parents have written him. He takes one out and reads part of it.*)

CLARA: But don't you stop writing. You hear?

JACK: We included a whole set of stationary in that box. Stamps, too. Maybe someday we'll be able to write you.

CLARA: I tried to explain to your grandmother what you're doing. And she kept saying, "Selfish. That's all it is, selfish." I don't think so. When you were growing up I used to say I would do anything to make you happy. Now I know that's true.

JACK: We kept watching until you disappeared. We caught the next flight out. Neither one of us cried. Try as we might.

CLARA: I won't cry for the living. Not anymore.

JACK: God only knows where you are tonight.

(RALPHY *continues on his way.*)

CLARA: But, we'll keep writing. So you keep writing.

JACK: God bless you, Ralphy.

CLARA: God bless you.

RALPHY: New Mexico. No, now I'm serious. Really. Or Palm Springs. Or Key West. Yeah, that's the beach for me.

(RALPHY *walks off stage past* CLARA *and* JACK.)

END OF PLAY

www.ingramcontent.com/pod-product-compliance
Lightning Source LLC
Chambersburg PA
CBHW070035110426
42741CB00035B/2788